Feelings

A collection of poems to relate to and encourage conversations and the sharing of feelings to develop deeper connections.

By

Alyce King

Dedicated to my mum for always standing by and to Ben for your patience and love.

"Still I rise…" Maya Angelou

Contents:

1. Inner Feelings
2. Save Us
3. Grief
4. Pearls
5. When I Fall
6. Guide
7. Lost
8. The Writer
9. Together
10. Healing Waters
11. Nature Gem
12. Picnic Bench
13. Summertime Sadness
14. Overwhelm
15. Yellow
16. Sea Soul
17. The Breath of Spring
18. Spring … Finally!
19. Let's Grow Old Together
20. Haiku: Forgive
21. Haiku: Enjoy
22. Trees
23. Word Play
24. Fireworks
25. Identity
26. Family Tree
27. The Whispers of Scars
28. Education
29. Mum
30. The Ending

Inner Feelings

Glittering sun rays brighten my day
whilst the rain washes away my soul
birds sing and lift my spirits,
take flight and look from above
into my life and how I live
notice what others see in,
sparkling waters glisten and calm
an anxiety ringing alarm
I sit at the water's edge
watching it constantly
swim further towards the sea
I breathe in the fresh, algae tinted air
and feel reset and ready to live, to care
for myself and others once again.

Save Us

I search for a different viewpoint angle
endeavouring to release our tangle
stretched time, depleted time
shows in our ability to chime read from the same page
and line
our backbone misaligned
irritation and inflammation
of our nerves, the smallest thing, the quietest comment,
the difference between content or sin.
None of it's intentional - we must learn to be better
humans
to one another and
as a team - communication
will ensure depth to our foundation.
Your view can differ from mine
it's okay, it's a sign of the times
but we need to link arms and
keep ourselves out of sinking sand.

Grief

a black wave washes over,
the solemn dong of a bell
icy, rain drip-feeds your soul
as bottomless as a well
no comfort from anyone -
no words can offer relief
though ten minutes ago you said you were fine
but here strikes again, this ugly, weighted grief.

River of Grief

Grief is a river;
trickling past those it does not dampen,
drowning those it soaks with a sudden splash.
Cold, waves continue to crash into your bones
never to disappear once announced to you.
Days will pass with a sad feeling but
bob along the water's rhythm,
then perhaps a song, a word, a memory, a picture
and the river will burst its banks, opening its floodgate.
Fast flowing, it can wash you out to sea,
once you are within the arms of the water,
you won't ever be free.
You find ways to cope, to manage, a new
normal you now learn to live, occasionally coming up
for air.
Someone with the freedom of carrying no grief,
never had that waterfall of sadness,
will never understand daily life
will never be the same again.

Pearls

Wisdom deep and understanding great,
Action sometimes ignores the rules of fate.
Little seed bombs within the ocean,
yet not contributing to pollution.

When I Fall

your hand stretches out
reaching for mine,
you pick me up
when I am down.
I make mistakes
you're my hero,
you pick me up
when I am down.
Wrong place,
or wrong time,
you pick me up
when I am down.
There aren't many who
would constantly pick up
like you do
when I fall
you're there,
your hand reaching out.

Guide

I hear you speak
when I'm feeling weak
encouraging me to be strong
delighting me with a song
You guide me to a better place
where I feel at last that I can face
the difficulties and the battles
and if I shake the world with a big enough rattle
I know larks will rise and sing
and my life will once again begin.

Lost

I hear you
I speak to you
and you guide me through the really bad times.
I smell you
I feel you
and you comfort me when I'm alone, confined.
I know you
I know your favourites
but you don't exist, you're a mime.
a sign, maybe
an imaginary friend, they say,
I'm mad - need help - or I'm
living a lie - grow up, you're an adult now,
but I know you, I know you're there.

The Writer

She sits facing the page
her face written with life lines and laughter
but holding the pen she has nothing to write -
nothing to share, nothing to say.
He taps away on his keyboard,
letters filling gaps on the page
his story isn't one of joy but it's his
to share, he has so much to say.
She meets him through a friend,
he talks, she listens
he lists his achievements without asking,
the envy rises, her determination fired up
ready to write her story, her version of events,
she has so much to share, everything to say.

Togetherness

quilting me with your conversation
mountains separate our views
yet our connection anchors us
as friends together we queue
for life to whisk us up and away
we celebrate our differences
though consider each person's faith
together we offer inference
to new life and to new ideas
responsible for one and all
minus any social isolation
conversation a possible fireball
division or separation no more
enlighten me with your life story
let me learn from your experience
let me honour and share your glory
feel peace and tranquillity
a creative space within
to share, connect and offer
simple help or check-ins
listen to the world's spoken word
join and belong with others
share sensitive empathy and
guardianship sincerely with one another.

Healing Waters

Emerald green and ocean blue
come together in a perfect hue
as you soak within you'll heal within
nurtured by nature's gin
a powerful mix of tonic and calm
its radiant shimmer, a hope glimmer
underneath face value of wet
a love laden button to reset
feel its arm around your shoulder
warmth, tender and comfort
it reaches for you when you need it
so listen then come to the edge and sit.

Nature Gem

I poke my finger into it - it ripples,
breaks the flow, though it just paddles
around, no meltdown, just adaptation -
over time it will erode these banks
of wildflowers and insects and bumblebees,
the course will change and it will tread
where it wants to go no permission needed
or given. I listen close, near a blackbird
sings soulfully, a grasshopper clicks hello,
a heron swoops low; the bailiff,
a warning sign. Then a swan, a natural beauty
floats past with her brood, gorgeous cygnets
learning life. Touch it and you connect - water
has been on Earth since day one, never losing
value, never losing strength, never losing vitality.
Water has importance; for you, for me, for them,
keep it clean, pollution free, forever a sparkling gem.

Picnic Bench

Sitting, wondering, what if, maybes, whys,
the questions sit comfortably, the thoughts edgy.
Sunshine catapulted onto my skin, bare,
touching it intensely, feeling heat, burn.
Gentle afternoons leading to evening
Watching families create memories,
couples lie talking, planning, children
playing with imaginary friends and stories.
I watch from my picnic bench, placed to the side
in full view, I sit with my thoughts
casting my eye around, noticing conversations -
witnessing arguments - catching connections,
though no one watches or hears me.

Summertime Sadness

Laugh until we cry,
the sun doesn't die,
watch the clouds disappear,
we live without fear,
trees bright green,
rumours mean,
Flowers burst out of nothing, tower,
don't you let them have power,
confrontation,
infatuation,
summertime sadness,
life goes on,
glaring moments within the heat
bring darkness, defeat.

Overwhelm

There's too much pressure here
I need to create space in my head, clear .
More demands flood in and
I compress as if within a tin,
I need space.
"Please?"
I hear, I curl, I crumble.
My plates are spinning too fast,
My head, my life is out of control.
Help...
Tears fall.

Yellow

Yellow splashes of sunshine
Pooling
Yellow drops of sunshine
Beading
Yellow dashes of sunshine
Quilting

Sea Soul

My wild sea soul's hair serpentines
waving, blowing in the wind,
A shiver across my skin,
Feet dug into the sand, into the Earth,
Sea salt sprinkled across my palate,
The icy waves lapping at my feet,
1… 2… 3…
A deep, sudden inhalation of breath,
A glow of cold catching my internal organs,
Slow, controlled breath exhaled,
Ready.

The Breath of Spring

The change from winter to spring is monumental,
yet it slips silently through the world.
The breath of spring, an inhalation,
as winter is expelled.
We lose the dark, the hidden, the sorrow of winter,
We gain the light, the brightness, the joy of Spring.
Though I feel we receive more and I wonder if you
agree?
Spring brings hope, it brings joy, it brings gratitude, it
brings strength.
Spring brings kindness, it brings empathy, it brings calm,
it brings time.
So when the winter air silently slips away to hibernate,
and the spring air awakens, let it guide you
to a better place, it'll put a smile upon your face.

Spring… Finally!

Blossom tinkers to the ground,
spring flowers no longer lost, but found,
warmer days,
sunshine rays,
bird song from dawn until dusk -
the Blackbird is proud to busk.
sunsets golden,
windows open,
welcome spring,
where have you been?

Let's grow old together

Let's grow old together,
until we're looking for the missing slipper,
retracing many steps for no answers,
searching for the pair of glasses that sit upon our nose,
From pint glasses to beakers,
Tractors to mobility scooters,
We'll be known as the 'two old farts on wheels.'
With waterproof mattress protectors, for accidents; anon.
Watch us shuffle hand in hand, to community coffee mornings,
armed with plenty "well, back in the day, when I was younger..." anecdotes to say.

Let's grow old together,
pottering in the garden, more frequent rests and cups of tea,
so toilet breaks more frequently.
Complaints it's too much, but not enough to give it up,
too stubborn to accept help.
Sitting in our armchairs, reading daily news,
probably still scrolling through,
reminiscing of the good times, yet still able to create new memories,
perhaps laugh at just how bad life got at times, yet here we are indeed.

Let's grow old together,
watching youngsters gesticulating at your driving, when
that was you just years ago.
Perhaps we'll find a joint hobby,
though I can't see what, not sure on bingo or knitting or
karaoke.

Let's grow old together,
make sure we spend the money, that you've worked hard
to earn,
even now there's still new things to learn.
You already care for me, but maybe one day I'll return,
the helping, the washing, and the joyous bum wiping,
we'll manage together,
so let's grow old together.

Haiku: Forgive

It's okay to say I
Forgive, but not quite forget,
Truth is brave, listen.

Haiku: Enjoy

Take the time, sip wine,
Eat the chocolate biscuit,
Or two, or the pack.

Trees

Because they work miracles;
dissipating pollution.
Because they improve well being;
mentally, physically, emotionally.
Because they remove co2 from the atmosphere;
photosynthesis changes it to oxygen.
Because they tackle climate change;
a storage tank for carbon,
Because they breathe life;
a natural filter for air quality,
Because they connect communities;
the lungs of our cities,
Because they are homes;
to wildlife, nature, declining species,
Because they defend;
against Floods and soil erosion,
Because they provide a roof;
shelter from weather, hot and cold, human or other,
Because we need trees,
End of.

Fireworks

He shouts,
she shouts,
we can hear them,
through the walls.

He's wrong,
she's right,
here we go,
another fight.

They take it in turns,
causing yet more burns,
a fireworks display,
yet there's nothing for us to watch or say.

There's more we can do
to look out and help others through
tough times or harsh realities
don't sit back and let it be.

Word Play

Natter, Natter,
Chatter, Chatter,
Words really do matter.

Listen, Listen,
Glisten, Glisten,
Imagine sound in your vision.

Read, Read,
Need, Need,
Fill your vocab up with greed.

Feel, Feel,
Real, Real,
Have empathy to heal.

You, You,
Meu, Meu,
Forever it will be us two.

- Meu = Me in Portuguese

Identity

Consider your identity,
Do you view it with positivity or negativity?
Is it a simplicity;
An agility of responsibility.
Does your identity hold you in captivity?
With little flexibility,
Mostly hostility?
What would it take for your identity to be your liberty?
Ban behaviour obscenity,
An elasticity of possibility,
Those near and far,
and within the vicinity,
Must make it probability,
An infinite certainty,
Accept our creativity,
To create serenity,
For equal identity.

Family tree

As you peel back the layers,
Discovering the past,
Understanding ancestors,
Reading memories of the family cast.

Finding out who came before,
Bringing their history to life,
Where in the world they came from,
Learning who became their wife.

Were they highly skilled or qualified?
Did they fight in a world war?
Or maybe they didn't work by choice.
Now you want and need to find out more.

Interesting, to scratch beneath the surface,
Of family history,
Teaching you and generations to come,
Just how, and who, you came to be.

The Whisper of Scars

It's a blunt reminder of perhaps a traumatic time. The scars may be visible, the scars may not be seen, but certainly felt.
Some scars are welcome; that scar may mean your baby survived, the scar may mean you survived. But even these can be tinged with guilt, sadness, pain or anger.
It's part of the healing process, to heal an injury, a wound or trauma.
The whisper of a scar may be private, or maybe the whisper spreads like wildfire, it becomes conversation.
The cause or place of the scar isn't a competition, all scars are equal: they show pain, emotions, healing and battles.
If you can't see the scar, be there, the other can see it, it is a constant reminder, you're the lucky one if you can't see it.
But, a scar, like the pain, will heal, and in time may fade, the conversation may silence, but it will never disappear completely.

Education

As adults we are encouraged to be unique,
Be who you really are,
Don't form to a crowd.
Yet our children are being educated,
With an education that only fits
One size and is rigid.
Let us be more open,
Accepting, and supportive,
There are more ways to learn;
Listen, do, watch, play.
Don't let those in offices get the final say -
If your child learns differently, be bold, be open,
Encourage them, support them and give them opportunities.
As adults we are encouraged to be unique,
As adults we need to encourage our children.

Mum

To grow up as your daughter,
I had freedom and a choice.
You guided me like a light,
Yet allowed me to have a voice.
Adventure days, I can't recall,
Ballet classes were a ball.
You supported me when it got tough,
Even with my regular slams and huffs.
So here are my adult thanks,
For all you've done, and all you do,
Your love always gets me through.

The Ending

Just in case when my time comes I'm not able to be articulate,
I may have lost my marbles, I may just deteriorate.
But I want the chance to thank you,
for the care, strength and love you have shared all our life through.
My rock, forever. I want you to know in case I can't say it,
hold my hand and you'll hear it anyway;
I love you.

Printed in Great Britain
by Amazon